KU-104-951

CREEPY CRAWLIES

This I-Spy book belongs to:

Stewart Burke

Earthworm
Everyone knows what an Earthworm looks like. Perhaps this is because the soil under 1 acre (0.4 ha) of grassland may hold 3 million of them!
I-Spy for 5

Roman Snail
Snails belong to a group of animals called molluscs. The Roman Snail is also known as the Edible Snail.
I-Spy for 50

Common Garden Snail ↑
Molluscs include some well-known sea creatures such as cockles, limpets, and even octopuses. The shells of most snails coil in a right-handed direction; **score double if you find a left-handed snail.**
I-Spy for 5

White-lipped Banded Snail ↓
The shells of land snails are made of a chalky material. They are usually found only in places where there is a lime-rich soil.
Where did you find your Banded Snail?

I-Spy for 15 Double with answer

Copse Snail

One of the uses of a snail's shell is to hold in water. In very dry weather snails can seal themselves into their shells. They usually only come out at night when it is cooler and damper.
I-Spy for 25

Hairy Snail

The 'foot' of a snail is so sensitive that it can even move over the sharp edge of a razor blade without cutting itself. **Where are the eyes on a snail?**

I-Spy for 25
Double with answer

Yellow Slug

Slugs feed by scraping away at the leaves, stems, and roots of plants using a rasp-like 'tongue' called a radula. Slugs and snails are very unpopular with gardeners.

I-Spy for 15

Black Slug

Because a slug has no shell, it loses water more easily than a snail. Therefore, slugs can not live in very hot or dry places.
Where did you find your Black Slug?

I-Spy for 15 Double with answer

Damselfly

Damselflies look like delicate Dragonflies. They can not fly so well as Dragonflies, and they rest with their wings held upright and touching.

I-Spy for **15**

Dragonfly

There are two main kinds of Dragonflies, often called 'hawkers' and 'darters'. The hawkers are more strongly built insects and fly well in pursuit of prey. The darters dart out from cover to seize an insect.

I-Spy for **15**

Mayfly

Most kinds of mayflies appear as adults (the winged insects) in May. They usually live long enough to find a mate — up to about four days only.

I-Spy for 25

Stonefly

Adult Stoneflies are always found close to water and, although they can fly, they often spend much of their time hiding under stones or among plants.

I-Spy for 25

Silverfish

Silverfish belong to an ancient group of insects called Bristletails. Silverfish often live in nooks and crannies in kitchens where they come out at night to feed on food scraps.

How do Silverfish get their name?

I-Spy for 15
Double with answer

Wood Cricket

Wood Crickets can
not fly and they live
on the ground in
woodland. They are
usually active
during the day.
I-Spy for **15**

Bush Cricket

Bush Crickets look like
Grasshoppers with
long feelers but they
are more closely
related to Crickets.
Bush Crickets usually
start to 'sing' in the
afternoon and carry on
into the night.
I-Spy for **15**

Grasshopper

Grasshoppers are
usually found in
grassland although
some kinds like peat
bogs. They 'sing' by
rubbing their legs
against a hard
vein on their
front wings.
I-Spy for **5**

Earwig

Earwigs get their name from the mistaken idea that they will crawl into people's ears. They do usually hide in small crevices and do not often fly — even though they can!

I-Spy for **5**

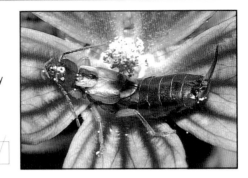

Shield Bug

Shield Bugs are shield shaped but some kinds are also known as 'Stink Bugs' because of the very strong and unpleasant smell which they produce. Bugs generally prefer dry conditions.

I-Spy for **20**

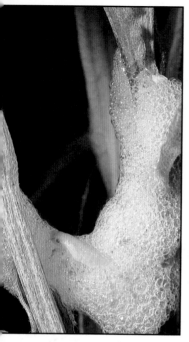

Froghopper

The Froghopper is a kind of bug. It is also called the Cuckoo-spit Insect because the young stop themselves from drying up by surrounding their bodies with a kind of froth. **Why should the froth be called 'Cuckoo-spit'?**

Ant-lion

Adult Ant-lions look rather like Dragonflies but they have club-shaped feelers. These insects get their name because of their fearsome young which feed on ants and other insects. Most kinds live in tropical areas but some are found in Europe.

I-Spy for 50

I-Spy for 10
Double with answer

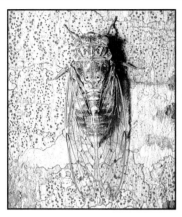

Cicada

Cicadas are rare in Britain. Most kinds live in trees. They 'whistle' or 'sing' by vibrating two flaps held in cavities on either side of the abdomen. You are more likely to hear them than to Spy them.

I-Spy for 50

Lacewing

Lacewings get their name from the network of veins in their wings. Although they look delicate, they have strong jaws and feed on aphids and other insects.

I-Spy for 20

Alderfly

Alderflies are found in large numbers in early summer on waterside plants, especially Alder trees. Like those of Lacewings, their wings have a network of veins.

I-Spy for 20

Swallowtail

This beautiful butterfly gets its name from the shape of its hind wings. The caterpillars of Swallowtails feed on the Milk Parsley plant.
I-Spy for **50**

Gatekeeper

The Gatekeeper Butterfly is quite common. It is also known as the Hedge Brown which suggests where it is most often to be seen.
I-Spy for **5**

Ringlet

Larger than the Gatekeeper, the Ringlet is another 'Brown' butterfly. It gets its name from the black and white circles on the undersides of its wings. **Why do many butterflies have 'eye spots'?**

I-Spy for **15**
Double with answer

Speckled Wood

The brown and yellow markings on the wings of this butterfly make it hard to see as it flits among the trees in woodland where the sunlight creates a dappled effect.
I-Spy for **5**

Marbled White

Despite its name, the Marbled White is a 'Brown' and is not related to the 'Whites'. It is found in rough pasture during mid-summer.
I-Spy for **15**

Fritillary

These butterflies get their name because the pattern of spots on an orangey back-ground looks a little like the Fritillary flower. Some kinds live mainly in woods while others are found in open country.
I-Spy for **15**

Tortoiseshell

There are two kinds of Tortoiseshell butterfly but the Small Tortoiseshell is more common. It appears in early summer and is often seen on the 'Butterfly Bush', the buddleia.
*I-Spy for **5***

Red Admiral

This large, brightly coloured butterfly is usually first seen in May or June but, although it is a Mediterranean insect, some individuals do manage to survive the harsh British winter.
*I-Spy for **10***

Painted Lady

This is another Mediterranean butterfly which travels to Britain in May and June. This brightly coloured butterfly lays its eggs on thistles and nettles.
I-Spy for 15

Comma

The Comma has tattered-looking wings for camouflage but it is the pale comma-shaped markings on the underwings which give this butterfly its name.
I-Spy for 15

Peacock

This large, brightly coloured insect may be seen during April and May and then again in September and October.

How does it get its name?

_____

_____

I-Spy for 10
Double with answer

Skipper

Skippers look more like moths than butterflies. They get their name because they beat their wings quickly and dart from place to place so they are hard to Spy.
I-Spy for 15

17

Common Blue

Blue butterflies are usually found on chalk grassland. Not all 'Blues' are blue, and the female Common Blue is a brownish colour.

I-Spy for **20**

Orange-tip

The Orange-tip is a member of the 'White' butterflies and it is easy to see how it gets its name. Don't forget, though, that female Orange-tips do not have the coloured tips to the forewings.

I-Spy for **5**

Large White

The caterpillars of Large whites will feed on plants of the cabbage family which is why they are sometimes called Cabbage Whites and why they are unpopular with gardeners.
I-Spy for 5

Clouded Yellow

In Britain, this is usually a rare butterfly but, from time to time, large numbers may migrate to Britain from continental Europe.
I-Spy for 25

Brimstone

This is another 'Yellow' butterfly and is often one of the earliest butterflies of summer sometimes emerging as early as February. The caterpillars feed on the leaves of the Buckthorn.
I-Spy for 5

Clearwing Moth

These moths get their name from their semi-transparent wings. They fly by day and, for protection, they mimic various kinds of wasps.

I-Spy for 15

Burnet Moth

This is another moth which flies by day. Their bright colours warn possible predators that their bodies contain a deadly poison. The caterpillars take in the poison from the plants on which they feed.

I-Spy for 10

Peppered Moth

The long, stick-like caterpillars of the Peppered Moth have three pairs of legs at the front of the body and four 'claspers' at the back with no legs between. They move by 'looping'.
I-Spy for **15**

Poplar Hawkmoth

As its name suggests, the caterpillars of this stout-bodied moth feed mainly on the leaves of Poplar trees. To avoid detection in the day, the Moth resembles a dead leaf.
I-Spy for **20**

Hummingbird Hawkmoth

The adult Hawkmoth hovers in front of a flower and uses its long coiled tongue to collect nectar. Some people actually think they have seen a Hummingbird when they Spy this insect.

I-Spy for **20**

Eyed Hawkmoth

The larva, or caterpillar, of the Eyed Hawkmoth has a flattened appearance which, with its green colour, makes it look remarkably like the leaves on which it feeds.

I-Spy for **20**

Buff-tip Moth

Buff-tip Moths hold their feelers pointing forwards when they are at rest. Because of their dull colours, they are sometimes called Smudge Moths.
I-Spy for **20**

Puss Moth

The caterpillar of the Puss Moth is green coloured for camouflage. If it is detected, though, it defends itself by squirting acid and by rearing up so that its false eye markings look terrifying.
I-Spy for **20**

Garden Tiger Moth

Tiger Moths taste unpleasant to birds, and the bright colours of the Moth's hind wings warn predators away. The pattern of the fore wings probably help to break up the insect's outline.

I-Spy for 15

Cinnabar Moth

The brightly coloured Cinnabar Moth gets its name from its red colour which is similar to that of cinnabar, an ore of mercury. These moths fly by day and night.

I-Spy for 15

24

Burnished Brass Moth

This moth is a member of a very large family of insects which all tend to have rather dull-coloured front wings.

I-Spy for **20**

Angle-shades Moth

Resting on the brown fronds of dead bracken, the dull colours and patterning on the forewings of this moth make it very hard for an enemy to see it.

I-Spy for **20**

Silver Moth

This moth is also sometimes known as the Silver Y — it gets its name from its colour and the Y-shaped markings on its wings. You are more likely to see the Silver Moth in June or July.

I-Spy for **20**

FLIES

Caddisfly
Caddisflies look rather like moths but they have hairs on their wings instead of scales. They feed on nectar and most kinds are active at night.
I-Spy for 15

Cranefly
Craneflies are sometimes called 'daddy-long-legs' and the weak-flying adults usually appear from late summer to autumn. If a predator grabs a leg, it breaks off to allow the insect to escape.
I-Spy for 5

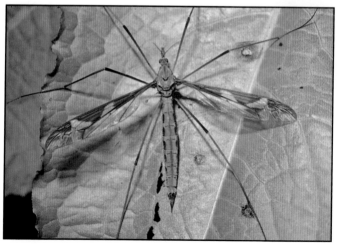

Mosquito

Small mosquitoes are often called gnats. It is the female which feeds on blood, usually that of birds. The males have hairy feelers which they use to 'hear' the wingbeats of the females.
I-Spy for **15**

Midge

This is a 'non-biting midge'. It gets its name because the adult flies do not feed. It should not be confused with the 'biting midges' which cause such irritation in parts of the Highlands and Islands of Scotland.
I-Spy for **15**

Horsefly

While male Horseflies feed on plant nectar, the females drink blood by biting animals including domestic cattle and humans. A Horsefly bite can be painful and will cause the area to swell.

I-Spy for **15**

Hoverfly

These wasp-like insects get their name for their ability to hover in the air. They can not sting, however, but their appearance fools their enemies into thinking that they are dangerous.

I-Spy for **5**

Bumblebee Hoverfly

This hoverfly looks like a bumblebee which allows the fly to fool bumblebees into letting it into the bee's nest to lay its eggs.

I-Spy for 15

Bluebottle

Male Bluebottles feed on nectar but the female often buzzes loudly into the house in search of meat on which to lay its eggs. These flies may spend the winter hiding in houses.

I-Spy for 5

Greenbottle

Like Bluebottles, Greenbottles are 'Blowflies'. If they lay their eggs on meat, the maggots burrow into the meat causing it to liquify — it is then said to be 'blown'.
I-Spy for 5

Dungfly

As its name suggests, the female of this bright-yellow furry-looking fly lays its eggs on cattle droppings. When they hatch, the grubs feed on the dung, helping to break down the manure.
I-Spy for 10

Robberfly

Robberflies feed by attacking other insects and sucking out the contents of their bodies. They have stiff hairs on their legs which help them to grip on to their victims.
I-Spy for 15

Scorpionfly

These insects are quite harmless despite their name which is derived from the appearance of the male. They actually eat plant sap and dead insects.

I-Spy for 15

Snipefly

It is generally thought that these rather wasp-like flies prey on other insects, and certainly their larvae do.

I-Spy for 20

31

Black Ant

Look for the Black Ant in your garden and do not forget that it is the female worker ants which have no wings; the Queen ant and the males have wings and can fly.
I-Spy for 5

Meadow Ant

This ant builds a mound in which it nests. Meadow Ants keep the eggs of aphids in their nest and, when the eggs hatch, the young aphids are kept in 'herds' like cows so that the ants can feed on the honeydew which the aphids produce.
I-Spy for 10

Wood Ant

Listen for Wood Ants as they rustle through the leaf litter on the woodland floor carrying bits of leaf and twig. Wood Ants will bite or squirt acid at attackers.
I-Spy for 15

Common Wasp

Common Wasps build nests made from a papery material which the Queen wasp makes by chewing up pieces of wood. In late summer when the colony breaks up, the workers search for sweet foods.
I-Spy for **5**

Hornet

Although these brown and orange wasps are bigger than Common Wasps, they are not usually aggressive and will rarely sting people.
I-Spy for **20**

33

Buff-tailed Bumble Bee

Bumble Bees live in smaller colonies than Honey Bees. Some workers suck up nectar while others collect pollen. As Bumble Bees pass from flower to flower, they pollinate the plants.
I-Spy for 5

Honey Bee

There may be many thousands of worker bees (females that can not breed) in one hive. The workers defend the nest and collect nectar which they feed to the bee grubs.
I-Spy for 5

Stag Beetle

This large beetle gets its name from the antler-like extensions to its jaws. Adult Stag Beetles do not usually eat. Stag Beetles can give a painful bite. **True or False?**

True

I-Spy for 15
Double with answer

Devil's Coach Horse

You are more likely to see this beetle at night unless you disturb one from under a stone. But beware, the Devil's Coach Horse is aggressive and can inflict a painful bite.
I-Spy for 15

35

Cockchafer

These large beetles usually emerge in May or June when they sometimes blunder into lighted windows. **What other common name is given to them?**

I-Spy for **15**
Double with answer

Soldier Beetle

Soldier Beetles prey on other insects which visit flowers but, probably because of their reddish colour, they are sometimes wrongly called 'Bloodsuckers'.
I-Spy for **10**

Dor Beetle
Dor Beetles feed on dung. The word 'dor' comes from an Old English word which means 'buzzing insect' or even 'bumble bee' and, when they are in flight, Dor Beetles do make a buzzing noise.
I-Spy for **15**

Ladybird
Everyone knows the Ladybird. There are different kinds with different numbers of spots. The bright colours warn enemies that they are unpleasant to eat. Ladybirds can also bite quite painfully.
I-Spy for **5**

Glow-worm

When is a worm not
a worm? When it is
a Glow-worm which
is a beetle. The
female looks like a
larva and she
glows to attract
a male.

I-Spy for 50

Woodlouse

Woodlice are not insects; they are related to crabs and lobsters.
During the day they hide in cool, dark places and come out at night
to feed. **How many legs does a Woodlouse have?**

I-Spy for 15 Double with answer ___ 16 legs ✓

Harvestman

Although they resemble spiders and are related to them, Harvestmen are not 'true spiders'. They are also sometimes called 'daddy-long-legs'.
I-Spy for **10**

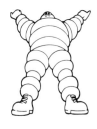

House Spider

Despite its name, the House Spider may also be found under logs and in holes in banks. Females are larger than males and may reach almost 2 cm (³/₄ in) in body length.
I-Spy for **5**

39

Garden Spider

This spider may vary in colour from black to reddish-ginger. It is found in gardens, woodlands, and heathlands. Look out for the rows of white markings which form a cross shape.
I-Spy for 10

Orb-web Spider

Orb-web Spiders get their name from the shape of the webs which they spin. In the case of this particular species, the web may be as much as 30 cm (1 ft) in diameter.
I-Spy for 10

Crab Spider

Crab Spiders are usually found on white or yellow flowers, and the females can change colour to match their surroundings. They lie in wait to catch their prey.

I-Spy for 25

Wolf Spider

These spiders get their name because it was once thought that they hunt in packs. They do run along the ground very quickly but they are not usually seen with victims.

I-Spy for 5

Centipede ↑
You can sometimes find centipedes hiding under stones or logs. Despite their name, which means '100 legs', they can have as few as 34 legs or as many as 300 or more!
*I-Spy for **10***

Millipede ↓
The difference between these creatures and centipedes is that, for each body segment†, they have two pairs of legs rather than one. Pill Millipedes roll into a ball when disturbed.
*I-Spy for **15***

Water Scorpion

The Water Scorpion can not sting but it can bite. Its name comes from the stinger-like spine at the end of its body which it uses as a kind of snorkel.
I-Spy for **15**

Pond Skater

The Pond Skater is also known as the Water Strider. The middle pair of legs is much longer than the others and is used to 'row' the insect across the surface of the water.
I-Spy for **15**

Water Measurer
This insect gets its name from the way it carefully walks along the surface of the water at the edge of a pond in search of the *Daphnia* on which it feeds.
I-Spy for **15**

Whirligig Beetle
These little insects get their name from their habit of moving around the surface of a pond at high speed. They feed mainly on other insects that have dropped into the water.
I-Spy for **15**

Dragonfly Nymph

This is the young of a Dragonfly. It is a fierce hunter and will use its extending jaws even to kill small fishes.
I-Spy for **20**

Marsh Wolf Spider

This particular kind of Wolf Spider is found in marshes where it eats the aphids that feed on duckweed.
I-Spy for **15**

Great Pond Snail

This snail can reach a length of 5.5 centimetres (over 2 in). Although most pond snails are plant eaters, the Great Pond Snail will use its rasp-like radula to scrape bits off dead animals.

I-Spy for 15

Freshwater Crayfish

Crayfish look like small lobsters and can grow to a length of about 10 cm (4 in). They live in clean streams and canals, and feed on snails, worms, and the young of insects.

I-Spy for 50

Adder

The Adder or Viper has a poisonous bite which is not usually fatal to healthy adults. Look for the dark zig-zag along the back and a 'V' or 'X' mark behind the head. Do not approach it closely.
I-Spy for **20**

Grass Snake

Grass Snakes can swim well and they are often seen by the sides of ponds, streams, or ditches. They hunt small creatures such as frogs or fish but the bite is not poisonous.
I-Spy for **20**

Slow-worm

This is sometimes called the Blind Worm. It is not blind, nor is it a worm, nor is it a snake. It is a legless lizard. Slow-worms live in damp places and feed mainly on earthworms.
I-Spy for **15**

INDEX

Answers

Hairy Snail: At the ends of the stalks on the snail's head.

Silverfish: From the coat of silvery scales which covers the insect's body.

Froghopper: Because the froth is usually seen at the same time of year that Cuckoos arrive.

Ringlet: Because predators sometimes attack the false eyes, and only get away with a small bit of wing instead of the whole insect.

Peacock: Because the spots on a wing similar to the Peacock's tail.

Stag Beetle: False. The Stag Beetle's jaw muscles are weak.

Cockchafer: Maybug.

Woodlouse: Ten.

© I-Spy Limited 1991

ISBN (paperback) 1 85671 007 6
ISBN (hard cover) 1 85671 008 4
Book Club edition CN1979

Michelin Tyre Public Limited Company
Davy House, Lyon Road, Harrow, Middlesex HA1 2DQ

MICHELIN and the Michelin Man are Registered Trademarks of Michelin

A CIP record for this title is available from the British Library.

Edited and designed by Curtis Garratt Limited, The Old Vicarage, Horton cum Studley, Oxford OX9 1BT

The Publisher gratefully acknowledges the contribution of Premaphotos Wildlife who provided all the photographs in this I-Spy book.

Colour reproduction by Norwich Litho Services Limited.

Printed in Spain.